LOOI
FROI

VERSE INSPIRED
FROM THE EARTH

Lin "Frog" Simmons

Hopper Expeditions

To Mark & Kath
My Friends
Forever
PEACE
Love,
Frog

ISBN: 0-9659925-0-0

Cover drawing by:
    Lin "Frog" Simmons

Edited by: Stephen Wylie

Printed in the USA

Hopper Expeditions
P.O. Box 52
Mokena, IL 60448

100% LIFE RECYCLED INTO VERSE
ON 100% RECYCLED PAPER

FOR

Steve, Derek
My folks, Al and Esther
Dee, Barry
Paula, Laura
Alex
Julie, Aunt Monie
Joel, Rick
Fred, Kris
Kindred Spirits
and
Jan's Spirit that lives on

ACKNOWLEDGMENTS

A very warm thanks to my husband Steve for his love and patiently waiting for a poet. To my folks for their love, encouragement and sense of humor. My sister, Dee for her love, wisdom and faith in me. My sister Paula for her love, faith and warm Motherly way. My sister Jan for her love, inspiration and teaching me her love of trees. My nephew Derek for his love and having faith in me. My sister-in-law Julie for her encouragement and appreciating my sense of humor. Dorothy Kavka and Wanda Johnson-Hall for their guidance, patience and humor. My brother Joel Jaskowiak for his Spirit, his Polish humor and buying the first book. Rick Russ for having faith in me and always using the key. Steve Jaskowiak for helping me out with Nellie both times. Fred and Kris Hahn for lending me their lily pads. The Wind, The Rain, A Beautiful Dance of Indian Summer, and Elaine Ruettiger for their wisdom and inspiration.

INTRODUCTION

"Looking At Life From A Lily Pad" looks at our diverse world in a simple way, because simple we are. From a butterfly to an ancient Redwood Tree, we are all brothers and sisters sharing life. None is more significant than another. And this beautiful Earth has inspired verse. I would like to share these poems with you, because without life's inspiration these pages would be empty.

PEACE

I wish I could go to an untouched place
To a beautiful wide-open space
Where there was never a quarrel
Or word spoke in haste
Never any sorrow or anger to taste

Could there be a place so kind
Where a quiet river winds
And peace fills the air
No sadness lives there
Where hate could not live
Would vanish through a sieve
Misunderstandings could not survive
Cause folks would be too wise

And all God's creatures would get along
Evening would set with a peaceful song
And at each glow of breaking day
Warmth would fill each heart to stay
To hold a warm bond as friends
And peaceful feelings each would send

Is there a place I pray I find
This peace of heart and unity of mind
For if Love it does exist
Then this place the angels kissed.

MARLEY CREEK'S BEGINNINGS

You start without warning
Beginnings are dawning
Your waters they lay
At peace on this day

But at times I'm perceiving
Their strength as their leaving
The banks to explore
And open new doors

Frogs they are singing.
Ducks happily winging
Though its shape is changing
As this journey you're arranging
On a Southwest streak
Marley meets Hickory Creek

And from there where you head
Of most it's been said
Is the city of New Orleans
The Mississippi has the means
To take in the waters
Sent by so many daughters

Eventually they meet
The Gulf and the heat
Of the South and its borders
Soon the Atlantic waters
And off to cause currents
And tropical turbulence

This peaceful scene to my West
A hurricane could some day invest
But here it lays a spark
For amphibians ducks and parks
Itself for a while
Seemingly mild
Nourishing this land
Late Summer's flowers they stand

So bright in their stay
Slowly part their way
Always leaving a few
Stragglers for memories to ensue
Until the cold comes along
She sleeps Winter long
Resting for her entrance
Again frogs she will send us

And though her journey it is long
Passing towns as she moves along
To me I shall perceive
Her as always in my dreams
Feeding life and nourishing the Earth
Never tires of her work
For the beauty she lay in her dawning
Sends a lifetime of hope calling

And the life she gives as she makes
                her Southwest journey
Is only a glimmer as her day it hurries
This peaceful existence she lay today
Will live on so many lifetimes away.

HICKORY CREEK IN THE WOODS

And when the sound of the jet
        had passed
All I could hear was the creek
        and a few birds calling
As my eyes
        they did cast
Upon the water I knew some
        from the Marley was falling

She moves so gently
        on her way
The Wind seemed to
        show her the way
And a squirrel playing
        near the shore
Searching hard for
        lunch he forged

The quiet of life
        on its journey
Is what my soul
        was yearning
And among the trees
        as I sit by the water
I found all those things
        I had lost earlier

A moment of desperation
      looking at the human race
This quiet waking beauty
      did erase
I found a place
      away from home
For when my body needs
      to roam

To feel the Earth
      beneath my feet
Perhaps some day
      a friend I'll meet
But for now
      this Hickory Creek and woods
Is a present God
      put underfoot

And this bridge over
      which I'll ride
To find what's on Hickory's
      other side
Will bring me back
      to the peace
That her rolling waters
      do release.

REFRIGERATOR POET

I'm a Refrigerator Poet
Yes I know it
I send these rhymes
To folks and most times
They land on the fridge
Magnets stuck to their edge
Sometimes they're taped
But their destination it's fate

They live on refrigerators
When hungry think of me with favor
Cause if I sent you a rhyme
Then you'll be on my mind
Because the message they send
My heart it did tend

And if by chance they fall to the floor
Please secure me to the door
Because if an ice box is my fate
That thought yes I can take
But crashed to the ground
Where feet they might pound
Or Jell-O may slither
And paper will wither
My heart's in these words
As this pen makes its turns
For your inspiration led me near
To these rhymes that I hear.

LIFE BRUSHING PAST ME

A dry leaf falls
        from the Maple Tree
And brushes against
        my arm to its peace
August has flashed
        before my eyes
Fall sends her message
        an entrance she tries

But Summer
        her short stay tries to hold
On to these moments
        as nature unfolds
Its never ending
        cycle of life
I only wish these warm days
        had more time

Cause the colors
        will change
And her face
        rearrange
This picture that
        stands before me
And the unpredictable
        Winter we'll see

A frozen sleeping world
　　　of desolation
Though Spring will bring it
　　　back to this destination
Then life again
　　　will abound
And peace and Love
　　　on the Earth will sound
To bring me back to
　　　these warm days
And the message the
　　　Earth relays

That life comes and
　　　it goes
When it's taken
　　　we never know
So enjoy the life around you
　　　on this fine day
And let your troubles
　　　go their way.

THE MESSAGE OF INDIAN SUMMER

Relaxing on this
     Indian Summer Day
No worries to get
     in the way
Pleasant winds from
     the Southwest
Are always a
     welcome Guest

The birds enjoying
     the morning
And leaves lay about
     to give us warning
That soon trees
     will be bare
Showing their
     Winter wear

And the morning song
     of birds
Will be only a refrain
     to be heard
Peace in leaving after
     work is done
Watching the southern
     journey of the sun

Can be felt by all
          on this Autumn day
As the sun stands alone
          and warms with her rays
Colors of green and yellow
          and brown
Are the pictures as
          I gaze around

Does nature feel
          sadness in parting
Or only complete with
          its disembarking
No the peaceful feeling
          of this day
Only reflects her
          resigning way

That the cycle
          has been complete
No need to regret
          retreat
Cause the life they've given
          will nourish next year
The generation to follow
          so near

Life in all forms
      takes new meaning
In this Indian Summer
      morning perceiving
She gives a message
      of hope for all life
Here for some reason
      we all hold a light

And as I watch those
      close to me
Part, it brings
      a sense of harmony
That their journey
      has been complete
No longer tread
      on their feet

But the nourishment and love
      in their stay
The Earth will always
      somehow portray.

LOVE AND WISDOM ON THE WIND

Oh Autumn
      with your natural beauty
You change life to its brilliance
      then you take it away

Your warm Winds are filled
      with the colors of fall
As we watch life part
      in a graceful way

You save some soon parting
      from the harshness of Winter
I've seen so many
      taken under your wing

Now the Wisdom and Love
      of ninety-two years is parting
Once again you've taken
      a product of Spring

I hear the warm
      Winds blowing
The night
      it is growing

Please hold proudly
      the beauty of this man
Riding on your Winds
      as they sail across the land.

JACK

You showed us
    your beautiful life
A new child
    before our eyes
Fighting for a
    chance to live
For a moment our
    hearts stood still

But thirty-six hours and
    a shining light
You are our third
    beautiful child
Made me wonder
    how it did feel
As the birth canal
    you did perceive

Then out into
    an unusual world
So different from
    surroundings you had learned
Was it an adventure
    as many we partake
In our lives
    numerous we make

Maybe for all the
    changes we endure
God gives you this
    first one to be sure
That the others
    will all seem easy
Life's episodes
    Mother Nature's character seasoning

Or could this sudden
    new adventure
Be like a first look
    at the Grand Canyon's center
Hearing it calling
    but unable to perceive
At last in awe
    by its grandiosity

Could ponder questions
    of life all day
No words to describe
    the happiness you gave
Another heart
    in our lives
With hope for the future
    and many miles

Can picture us son
    golfing some day
But for now it's enough
    that in my arms you lay.

THANKSGIVING

Thanksgiving is a time
      to give thanks for our lives
For visions we perceive
      and dreams that survive
We are thankful each morning
      for the break of day
And inspired by a sunset
      as nature plays

But we choose one day
      of the year
To be thankful with
      those who are dear
Though some folks we love
      may be out of sight
In our hearts on this day
      they show light

Celebrations for all
      they may vary
Though close to our hearts
      we will carry
A feeling of peace
      as we partake
For whatever God's given us
      we choose to celebrate

And thankful most for
      the intangible things in our souls
Gifts we're given
      that make us whole.

I'LL TAKE ONE COMPUTER PLEASE
AND MAY I SPEAK WITH A TREE

Computers
  I'll take a couple gigabytes
Ah, throw in two more
  why fight
Speed and Memory
  we are seeking
Though this computer language
  they are speaking

Doesn't mean
  much to me
My instincts
  they flee
When they speak
  of RAM
How much would you like
  MA'AM

Whatever you think
  I need
And do I have
  to feed
This computer
  you're putting together
Does it mind
  stormy weather

And is there
  a guarantee
Will it drive me
  to insanity

OK
        figure the price
And if I ask
        really nice
Will you
        throw in a mouse
My cat's cleared
        out the house
And software
        I'll have that installed
You say you'll have
        to make some calls

Shopping
        I've never enjoyed
So much to choose from
        it gets me annoyed
So over the phone
        I'll try
To find the best computer
        to buy

You sound pretty
        at ease
Your honesty
        it does please
Me
        so I'll take one
Computer
        and hope I can get it to run
Ah, the age of technology
I relate better to a tree.

SLUE FOOT

Although I cried
      when you died
I wonder what it
      must have felt like
To live in that
      tired old body of yours

Marked with age
      history's page
Though slow of pace
      it moved with grace

As Winter neared
      your time was here
Your legs couldn't hold
      a body so old

So you lay down to rest
      on a crisp Autumn nest
Never to rise
      though your body still tried

I begged you to stay
      as you gave your last day
My eyes filled with tears
      your memories still here.

NEW VOICES IN THE WIND

I stopped to hear
      your leaves rustling today
Knowing that
      on the Earth they lay
But a habit is hard
      to break
As these late Fall days
      they take

The life we are accustomed
      to feeling
We watch them
      fleeing
But I always hope
      for one last dance
Of your music
      just one last chance

But the Wind blew
      strong and I heard
You speaking
      could feel your words
As in a whistle
      not your usual sounds
And your beauty
      it did surround

Standing tall and bare
    in a cold gray sky
As Winter's entrance
    she did try
And at last I found
    a way to listen
To your wisdom in
    Winter's prison

And alone I will
    not feel
As Winter she does
    steal
The sounds of a
    day full of life
As with her cold
    she divides
The life we're used
    to perceiving
With her approaching
    it is retrieving

And the cold of
    Winter's stay
Will feel warmer to me
    from this day.

FIRST SNOW

The first snow of the year
Rests peacefully on the trees
And anything you may fear
Is covered by its silent beauty

A walk on the first bed of snow
Is something of which I know
Warms the heart as it gently lands
On your coat and hat and covers your hands

Boots they make their way
As this covering makes you play
Tricks with your different steps
Slippery heavy and very wet

But more is seen on a
            slow moving morning
Though nature is covered
            perceiving its longing
For sleep after
            achieving its work of three seasons
A white blanket covering trees
            is pleasing
To the eye as its brilliant
            fall colors have parted
And new buds on their
            limbs have started

Does a tree feel the cold of
      the snow through its bark
Or does this outer layer
      keep it apart
From the elements that
      cross our lives
We know Mother Nature
      sometimes she pries

Into our souls as she
      plays her games
Though we try without luck
      her ways to tame
Snow plows and warm homes
      keep us going
But on our being her nature
      it is showing
Tired eyes and early nights
      of sleep
Hard to rise as the
      sun does peek
Cause cold days are
      for inside
Ask any bear as in
      the Winter he hides

No we find ways
      around the elements
Snow tires boots and
      heating bills we're sent
While the tree stands tall
      and strong outside
Waiting for the Spring
      Winds to ride
To fill her branches
      with green again
And bring back home
      her feathered nesting friends.

A SPIRIT IN MY HEART

I keep seeing your Spirit
Dancing happily no fear in it
Is it you I see
Or my eyes playing games
Can you still be with me
Or a mirage to ease pain

So many miles we walked
And all of the hours we talked
Mostly without saying a word
Through our eyes our voices could be heard

Those sparkling eyes and endless smiles
With a Spirit you could not disguise
I call your name
Is it a game
Or do you hear my voice
Are the visions somehow your choice

The days grow long
I picture a smile that's gone
Is it you I feel in my heart
We always said we'd never part.

SNOW'S CHARACTER

Lying softly on their limbs
A beautiful image you give
Peaceful bright and determined
I watch as you are turning

A desolate Winter land to bright
Your white cover everywhere in sight
Gray fields come to life
And evergreens laugh at your plight

Do you know each others Spirit
Seems your personalities they fit
One tired and slumbering from Winter's stay
And then you make your entrance to play

With every object you can find
To its size you pay no mind
Cause tiny though you each may be
Together you work as a family

Descending on all things revealed
'Til most you have concealed
And when your work is done
An appearance from the sun
To show your brilliance as it lay
On this cold spot of Earth today

And again when warm air it peeks
Through the ground you will seep
Nourishing the life around
Silently you make no sound

So when Spring comes our way
Life will leave its slumbering days
And remember your peaceful stay
The love and brilliance you brought their way

Smiling in the warm sun
As Spring has taken your work and run
With sprouts of green and buds bursting
Flowers they will soon be thirsting

And in their minds they'll remember your gift
A warming blanket as you peacefully sit
Upon this Earth in Winter's voyage
'Til Spring she begins to edge
And changes your texture 'til none can be seen
Just water flowing as a stream

Snow yes I believe you have character
From the sky you float and then land here
Changing as your life it grows
Finally nourishing roots down to their toes.

FEBRUARY'S REIN

The Wind she howls
        this day grows cold
Rain it pours
        its mission untold
And soon these skies
        will turn their face
From her this rain
        will lose its place

To a frozen world
        of snow and ice
February holds
        a price
But never dull
        she changes scenes
Sometimes acting
        so serene

But we know her plight
        we won't escape
Her fury when she
        decides to take
Those cold winds
        from the North
And sends them knocking
        on your door

Covering what seemed
      so serene
Turning life as
      if you dream
But beauty she sends
      in spite
Of her fickle ways
      in plight
Cause variety she wears
      in her short stay
February's twenty-eight
      sometimes the longest days.

VACATION

With Kaopectate, Maalox
     and Alka-Seltzer in hand
We watched the waves
     roll up on the sand
And it was a refreshing change
     having men wait on me
But somehow I was unaware
     I ordered sushi

The Marguerites were
     very smooth
They certainly helped
     when my spouse wore snorkeling shoes
There was no need to get around
     in a rent a car
The "bus drivers were hell bent
     on death" but they'd take you far

And after enjoying
     six days in the sun
Our seventh day on the beach
     our skin got overdone
Ah, vacation
     I'll take one when I can
But for our next excursion honey
     I'll make the plans.

HARD ROAD TO PEACE

Meteors
      the Ice Age and Humans
They all had a
      way of doing
Harm to the
      life on this Earth
Sent her starting over
      as from birth

Yes we are just
      another device
That may not be
      so wise
We take from this
      planet all her beauty
For selfish gain
      as we are undoing

Everything God has
      put in our sight
Somehow it just
      wasn't quite right
We changed the
      direction of water
Our children only know
      what they're taught here
And we grow farther from
      this land
Take little time
      for where we stand

So little do we
    know
But our knowledge
    we always grow
Perhaps days were
    more at ease
When with our surroundings
    we were pleased

And changes to
    this Earth
Never came
    we loved her dirt
If Peace in getting along
    with our brothers
Is all in life
    we chose to discover
Our minds would
    so expand
We'd get along
    on this beautiful land

A ray of hope
    comes to mind
Maybe our destination
    we will find
This long hard wrong
    road we travel
May some day
    unravel

But from our journey
       we'll learn of life's pleasures
Cherish this Earth
       and live with her treasures
And the Earth
       will smile and heal
Humans who survive this travesty
       will feel

For the love of
       our brothers
Will cause harm
       to no other
And a smile this
       Earth will wear
As we handle
       it with care
No perhaps this hard
       road is what we need
So in the end with
       the Earth we'll feel.

EXTENDED VACATION

The conveyor moves
     round and round
Everyone else
     they have gone
But me I stand less and less
     patiently waiting
Wayward luggage
     I'll soon be claiming

I know it's hard
     to come home
After on an adventure
     you've roamed
And luggage with a
     mind of its own
Has tendencies to
     venture on alone

My favorite shirt was
     in that bag
And yes there was an
     identification tag
Maybe I'll check the
     conveyor again
Perhaps it's back
     was just visiting a friend

Oh there it is
        my eyes they strain
But a closer look
        no it's a game
That luggage plays
        with your eyes
For fun
        they can disguise

So you say you'll
        give me a call
And when it shows up
        you'll deliver it all
OK well I guess
        I'll be going
But somehow it's not
        secure knowing
My stuff is in
        another city
Perhaps still in flight
        drinking champaign and giddy

I know I don't take you
        out often enough
And your life in the attic
        is sometimes rough
But please come home
        tonight
I promise once in a while
        I'll let you outside

To sit
> on the deck
And fix you a drink
> what the heck
I'll fill you with all
> those things you like to hold
And shine you up
> so you look a little bold

Then home and waiting
> for a call
Perhaps my luggage
> it did fall
Off a carrier
> and on the runway
Maybe a plane will
> crush it suddenly

Ring
> oh I hear a bell
My luggage has arrived
> they tell
You'll deliver it
> in the morning
Tucked in for the night
> you hear it snoring

Thank you for finally
> finishing your journey
I know I shouldn't
> have worried
Cause vacation is hard
> to leave behind
Those days are just
> so hard to find.

PLANTING A SEED

We planted a seed
        on this warm Winter day
In hopes its life would
        always stay
But roots it must first learn
        to grasp
The Earth in order for
        life to last

And then as it shows
        its head in Spring
As birds return on wing
        they sing
A chance of survival
        they hope to attain
As they enter life's
        changing game

And once strong it will
        hold its place
Find love and life
        in its space
The seed that once
        had dreamed
Of life
        has now seen

Youth and the promise
      of time
With its new found
      strength it will find

A beauty so long
      dreamed
And heart warming
      life so real
From the seed of friendship
      planted before Spring
And all the happiness
      it does bring.

SIGNIFICANCE TO MAKE A DIFFERENCE

Your face is so young
Life has barely begun
But soon it may cease
War in your land has released

Running with no where to go
Food and water you'll never know
Those before you were not so wise
So your life will be short in size

A crying hungry painful face
A member of the human race
They say eighty-thousand people will pass on
The thought is staggering no battle won

Is there a way to end this poverty
Of spirit and body to set them free
I fear there is no end in sight
Though I search hard for that light

And here in the U.S.A.
Some folks complain for wanting each day
For more than they really need
One hour in a war-torn country and they would see
That their life is not so bad
They'd enjoy the fruit of this land

Though perfect our ideas are not
But food and a roof on top
Are gifts in this world so rare
Even American streets the homeless wear

So I thank God for my life
And nourishment to help me survive
Instead of wanting for more
Perhaps a gift to homeless and those at war

Because though just one person
If each acted to help another it would fill
The world with less hunger and more love
Maybe put a roof above
A family in need of a home
So no longer they'll need to roam

Can we with a home and food learn to share
To help the less fortunate with burdens they wear
Yes one person can make a difference
If each person makes an effort significant.

HOLDING ON TO A LIFE

You hang waving lightly
    in a morning breeze
Your youth shows
    but early you retrieved
And your family
    won't let you go
Holding on
    this love they show

But your mission
    was complete
Passed on
    your life did retreat
And it made me wonder
    how a journey is decided
Upon this Earth
    our circular ride

Some lasting years
    others only days
This picture of life
    we are portrayed
And I watch them
    hold your memory tight
Your early departure
    somehow wasn't right

But a vision of life
        you gave in your short stay
Touching so many
        and now on your way
Reasons for our
        span of life
Stand barren
        before my eyes
New life showing
        where others had parted
Journeys and roads pass my eyes
        they dart

And I looked again
        and saw your beauty
Shining through the eyes
        of those you did see
Then I knew your stay
        was not short lived
You filled your time here
        the love you did give
And peace came from
        your journey
No your life wasn't
        taken too early.

BOND BETWEEN THE SKY AND EARTH

Soaring high above
    the land
You shine
    in the morning sun
And from this place
    where I stand
Your work seems
    never done

But joy you must
    feel in flight
With this Earth
    below in sight
Effortlessly gliding
    circling high
Your life above
    the ground is mine

But somewhere in between
    we're joined
Cause from your visits
    you bring me joy
Do you watch for
    me to journey out
Then begin
    to circle about

I always thought
      my eyes saw first
But now I feel
      my heart does thirst
For your friendship
      and I sense your presence
Through our hearts
      we both do sense

This bond for life
      we will always hold
The journey of our friendship
      the stories told.

NO PICTURES PLEASE

Yes they can scan
      your bones
And drink a liquid
      that makes you glow
Pictures they will
      deliver
Of any organ including
      your liver

But I say
      please keep your lens cover on
I prefer not to know
      what is found
Inside this body
      in which I live
Or any part that I
      may need to give

A little medication
      to
Or more attention
      I should pursue
To my heart or bones
      or any part
Please don't even
      start

I'm happy living in
        this human body
And I find it very
        calming
Not knowing what
        goes on inside
This life long journey
        my arteries do ride

Yes save that film
        for someone who might
Want to find a reason
        to fight
What's going on
        inside of them
I like to think of this
        shell as my friend

And when I pass on
        please no probing
Just burn to ashes
        scatter them knowing
I lived the best I could
        in here
Never worried of my mechanics
        not a fear

Yes your brain can
        keep you so long going
If of your insides
        you're never knowing.

ROOTS AND LIFE

As a child you dreamed of
        someday being a tree
At the age of seven the
        idea seemed funny to me

But years have gone by
I look to the sky
See branches waving high
And know you must have been so wise

Cause Roots and Life
        the picture they portray
An example I hold
        in my heart to stay
When I see them dance
        in the breeze
And change their wardrobe
        as seasons release

I wonder if they
        ever tire
Of their roots
        this circle of life
No their beauty in the
        birth of Spring
And Autumn's display
        the colors she brings
Before you sleep
        for the Winter days
In preparation for
        life to engage

Then your buds
        grow in size
Soon small leaves
        before our eyes
And with life in
        full display
On Summer's
        endless days
Seems its Spirit
        will never end
Until the message
        Autumn sends

And though we hate to
                say good-bye
This beauty before
        our eyes
Her parting is always
        made easy
With Indian Summer's
        warm breezes

All life must
        take a rest
In all seasons
        you give your best
What more can we ask
        of life
The message of a tree
        forever wise.

STANDING AS A TREE

Its beauty of life is always changing
Picture is always rearranging
But always eye appealing
Never a harsh image revealing

And beauty takes on new meaning
When a Tree perceiving
No need for material woes
Its needs for life it grows
Capturing each day for its worth
Portraying beauty from birth

And a distant memory of a young life
Stands before my eyes
Looking so full of beauty
As this image that stands before me

And sadness fills my soul
That so young she had to go
And I hope as a Tree she stands
In a quiet peaceful land.

BREAKFAST OF LOVE AND RESPECT

Love and Respect
      they reciprocate
When none is given
      we close a gate
Can't seem to get
      the feeling back
Harsh words
      they just attack

But there's a key
      to open the gate
Use it
      don't hesitate
A peaceful word spoken
      is all you need
That kindness shown
      will plant the seed

And Love and Respect
      will reciprocate
Grows with strength
      as if you ate
A chunk of Love
      in your breakfast
It will travel on
      in your Heart it will set

And soon the wrong
      has cleared the air
Respect and Love
      at you they stare
Nothing found in this world
      without giving
There's a life full of happiness
      worth living.

FREE FLOWING SENSATION

I followed the voice of
        the winding creek and road
They told me not
        to hurry
The miles and trees
        they did unfold
Their message was
        not to worry

Cause as you see before
        your eyes
The road and creek ahead
        they wind
They'll take you
        where your life should be
Give them time and
        you will see

The creek it doesn't
        know its destination
Keeps moving along
        a free flowing sensation
And again my life
        felt so right
This gray day with
        Winter's work in sight

Shed so much light
        again I could see
Keep moving along this winding road
        let my Spirit flow free.

SPIRITS MEET

So many Spirits
      touch us in this world
So fortunate I am
      to have heard
The sound of their hearts
      when we met
Because to a journey of friendship
      they led

And brought me more
      than I'd dreamed
With their faith and friendship
      they've made me believe
That Love it lasts
      through time forever
Spirits joined
      can never sever

Only things we touch
      can part
Don't know when the Spirit
      does start
But it remains and
      makes ties
This intangible part
      it survives

Through the ages
      and keeps hold
So much it has
      told
Of all the life
      it has known
The time it has
      grown

Moving onto new
      explorations
Experiencing new
      sensations
But remaining still
      the same
Though form
      it may change

And as we meet
      and I look in your eyes
Something inside me
      it tries
To know how we
      bond so fast
Was it a journey
      from the past

But wonder
        is all I can do
No answer
        will ensue
Do we really
        need to know
If these eyes
        they show

Another time
        another place
Only a figure
        was erased
No
        only this moment holds tight
What is in our
        sight
How we arrived
        a mystery
But the warmth I receive from you
                will always follow me.

IDA'S LOVE REMAINS
AND DESTRUCTION'S INSIGHTS GAINED

Ida sat at her husband's
    side
She turned down a chance
    to ride
In a life boat away
    from doom
The Titanic would be
    history soon

Some escaped the
    sinking ship
But most drown
    their fate did sit
With the cold icy
    Atlantic waters
And the destiny human arrogance
    brought there

But strong Love and
    tragedy
They brought to mind
    life's direction to me
Because it seems
    most change comes
From disaster as
    it's on the run

Some for good and
   some for worse
This part of life
   it seems a curse
That we gain insight most
   from grief
In her time
   she seems to speak

The loudest and clearest
   to us all
Unfortunately some
   have to fall
And life teaches
   so much from her stay
The aftermath has
   so much to say

And as I look at the
   shape of our Earth
I wonder if all this
   pain is worth
The knowledge we
   will some day gain
Cause very soon
   we'll feel the rain

As this life
  we've grown to know
Suddenly takes back
  control
And leaves only a
  little life showing
But Love from these children
  will be growing

Cause so much disaster
  will have to strike
For humans to finally
  open their eyes
Cause all the wrongs
  we are pursuing
Will take a miracle
  for any undoing

Many laws they made
  at sea
After the Titanic
  met her destiny
As many laws we will
  surely know
When Mother Nature
  puts on her show

To rid herself of
        all our mistakes
An immense change
        it will take
And I hope a few humans
        will remain
Who from our destruction
        will have gained

Insight into the
        beauty of life
As was the Love of Ida
        the devoted wife
Yes Love and destruction
        the strongest forces
On this Earth as she
        charts her courses

And I hope the strong
        Love of Ida is what is gained
When on this Earth only a
        few remain.

PRESENCE OF THREE

Spring's entrance
       a Comet and a Full Moon
I know folks will be
       crazy as loons
And I enjoy those days
       of nature's roll
Their cosmic powers
       they do pull

Tight on this old
       Mother Earth
We find ourselves
       drawn with her dirt
By these lunar
       experiences
And the sun
       as she peers

Straight down on
       the equator
On her center
       layers
And a visitor
       to our sphere
She makes a pass
       so near

We look for her
        light
In the stillness
        of night
And hope with
        skies clear
Her picture will
        draw near

Cause what
        do we know
Except this Earth
        where we grow
So when visitors
        arrive
We treat them
        so kind

Cause much we
        can learn
From this Earth
        as it turns
But a guest who
        comes so close
We must play
        perfect hosts

Cause so much
      learned from living
And when a chance for new ideas
      is given

We grasp them
      with hope
That something
      they will hold
Will lead us to
      an understanding
Of this place on Earth
      where we're standing.

ROBIN KNOCKING AT MY DOOR

The first day of Spring
  and a Robin is knocking at my door
The Vernal Equinox
  never know what she has in store
New life and hope
  on its way
Love in my heart
  is here to stay

Sunshine and these
  skies so blue
This picture of life
  comes shining through
Every day a
  new adventure
As each new piece
  the Earth sends here

Geese flying
  I hear them call
Two more enter
  their flight's so tall
Every bird
  has a song to sing
A future generation
  they will bring

Busy with life
      each day holds
The promise
      that nature's told
Hope
      it is strong in the air
In each swollen bud
      it does stare

Spring she brings
      back the life
That's been resting
      for a while.

YOUR FRIEND THE WIND

I just hoped I could hear you one last time
      whispering in the Wind
See you swaying with your Spring colors
      dancing in the Wind

But man has moved his dynasty
      closer to your arms
They say you're in the way
      you'll do humans too much harm
I watch you as your buds appear
      do you know your destiny
Can you feel their heartless words
      deciding on your right to be

Tomorrow they will make their judgement
      if your life will cease to be
But you've given so much life
      your Spirit will live on
Your friend the Wind
      has planted life your Seeds.

FIRST FROG OF SPRING

The first Frog of Spring
This morning his voice does sing
As ducks they waddle and swim about
This lone Frog his voice sings out

And brings the promise of new life
In search of courtship's delight
He knows Spring is in the air
And soon life will be everywhere

With his friends their voices join
With the thaw her days rejoice
Finding Love and the promise of Spring
To bring them back to this chorus they sing
Their voices gather all night long
Their serenade a Love song

And the simplicity of their life
Brings the joy of living to mind
Yes the Frogs they always bring
The hope for tomorrow as they sing.

A STORM WITHOUT WATER

Hail, lightning, rain
    Mother Nature brought us a storm last night
Her Children stood their ground
    some took shelter from her plight
But those rooted
    in their fields
Held their ground
    they would not yield
And the sunlight of the morning
    left birds singing
And a Frog's chorus
    replaced the storms retrieving

So much a storm can bring
    in its unpredictable stay
Somehow the next morning
    the rain it's given relieves the pain
But the storm caused
    by a human travesty
Leaves only mourning
    the day blinding unable to see

In Oklahoma
>   where storms take flight
A year ago
>   Humans turned the day to night
Sunny skies turned to
>   dark and dismal days
From a bombing
>   a Human's senseless ways

So as they gather
>   respect for Human tragedy
I look at how
>   these humans changed life so rapidly
They left no water
>   to nurture God's life that remained
Only buried corpses
>   a memorial field proclaims.

PARTLY SUNNY

I asked you if you had connections
If you could make the Sun come back to us
And at that moment it did shine
Though briefly I had to squint my eyes

Your Red Rock glistened
        and your flowers showed hope
Of a relentless cloud cover
        that we hold
Do you know who to ask
        can you change these ways
Bring us warm dry and
        sunny days

Or were you teasing with that
        brief morning glow
Is there a reason for this
        gloom we must hold
Sad faces and
        wet places
Please bring us more than
        Sun in small traces
The cold of the Winter
        we must bear
No Spring in '96
        and now no Summer wear

God, please stop teasing us
    with sunny forecasts
Are you tampering with
    the weather maps
My eyes are sore from
    lack of light
Please make these clouds part
    and skies so bright

Oh, I see
    it's only weather
And it'll build character
    in us forever
If we all don't first
    lose our minds
Our sense of humor
    is on the line

Please stop this teasing
Let the Summer release things
Like flowers and sun and warm breezes
Take away this weather that brings on sneezes

So much I ask
    a silly human am I
Thinking you will somehow
    listen and clear the sky
But without faith and hope
    what do we have
A silly human pointing at a
    Weather Map.

BROTHERS SHARING THE RAIN

You climb from your bed
     and spread your wings
This morning as the unceasing
     rain sings
Ducks they splash
     where dry ground lay
Of this storm
     they make it play

And down the creek
     where your waters flow
Dashing happily
     as you go
You enjoy
     the time to flee
From your banks
     you set yourself free

No boundaries
     to stop you today
Not with the
     love of the rain
She quenches your thirst
     and off you roll
A quiet creek
     she shows her soul

And life around her
      dances in glee
In her journey
      they believe
Because all children
      of the Earth
Brothers and Sisters we're
      tied from birth

So we smile when a brother
      shares his wealth
That Mother Nature
      has dealt
Cause share
      we will do the same
When our life flourishes
      from the rain.

SEASONS' NAMES

Why does Autumn
      have so many names
Perhaps it's because of
      her many changes
The leaves parting
      gives the name Fall
As we watch its ending
      call

And Spring she starts
      so barren
No camouflage she
      is wearing
But we watch her
      through her many changes
Every day her life
      it ages

But Spring
      it stays the same
We know her by
      one name
As a friend
      we watch her grow
But her name
      we always know

Perhaps we find
    a need
As Fall's days
    they proceed
To reason with the
    passing of life
So by changing her name
    we deal with strife

Can't say I really
    know
But as this Spring day
    grows
I know it only has
    one name
And by Fall
    life will be passing again

Many names
    I will be searching for
Because on a life
    God may close the door.

A TEN THUMB DAY

Was one of those
       ten thumb days
Who would have known that morning
       I'd travel this maze
When pieces of life
       fell through my hands
And in the paths I walked
       boulders would stand

Now the sun it shines
       on another morning
And I'll erase
       this memory's storming
Of obstacles and life
       and nature's way
That make you appreciate
       the other days
When thread easily
       slides through the needle
And people smile and
       I'm not so feeble

So many fascinating
       peaceful days
Cross my mind as I
       strive not to decay
From a ten thumb day
       and drenching rain
I'm still hanging on
       somehow not insane.

SETTING YOUNG WINGS FREE

A Baby Robin
        caught in a spot
Unable to free himself
        I helped him out
He sat and wondered
        what to do
He didn't know
        he could get through

Then I approached
        his resting place
He flapped his wings
        and off in space
Surprised he could fly
        he'd been held down
A young hearted Soul
        sent him off the ground

He flew and soared
        and flapped his wings
This morning I believe
        I could hear him sing
Not knowing he could
        fly again
A new journey
        he did begin.

ENDLESS SPIRIT

I know I've seen
    that smile before
Walking through
    my kitchen door
Eyes glowing and a
    Spirit so alive
Love and Laughter
    in his eyes

Passing through life
    so many things we bring
And work we've done
    who will keep
Our mission alive
    after we're gone
Afraid our work of life
    will be done

But product of our labors
    is not what matters as much
The Love your Spirit instills
    upon this Earth will always touch
And as I watch your son's eyes
    shining so bright
I know your beautiful Spirit
    will always be alive.

RAIN OF LIFE

You must have felt the
      coming rain
Cause the prior day
      your seeds you set free
Drifting peacefully
      life's refrain
So wise you are
      aged tree

And to my good fortune
      I was passing by
As your seeds
      through the air did fly
Gracefully dancing
      to the ground
In this peaceful rain
      I was found

Smiling as the hope of life
      surround me
A Mother
      sowing her seeds
With the chance
      for survival
To the Earth
      landing softly on arrival

Their wing carried them
           through the Wind
God in his wisdom
           did send
This sail to carry them
           gently on a breeze
A last look at
           their Mother tree

And I wanted to
           plant every one
In the warm afternoon
           sun
But I knew it was not
           their fate
Thousands flying
           cause only a few will make

A tree
           so strong and giving
The beauty they show
           in living
The Mother knew only few
           would survive
On this Earth
           as they did arrive

So she planted
        so many
Seeds of life
        she was sending
In hopes that a few
        would root
And send up
        a shoot

A sapling
        she could smile upon
As the summer
        donned
Itself with Spring's
        desires
For continuation of life
        she aspires

Life
        seen in its simple beauty
From a showering
        of seeds
So lucky I was
        to feel their journey
As a Mother
        planted her seeds.

SAFE WITH THE LORD

A prisoner of war
      he was trapped
But his Spirit
      it was free
Though life in front of him
      was unmapped
He had eyes
      to see

You see freedom
      is a state of mind
At peace with
      who you are
Inner contentment
      you will find
A heart of Love and respect
      will take you far

Though some may say
      "Join, we'll set you free
And keep you
      safe from harm"
Freedom you will
      never see
Just violence and
      arms

The Lord will hold
      you safe
Believe in his Love
      and life
His own life
      he gave
Still today
      his Spirit flies

Faith and knowledge
      are freedom
Don't ever lose
      your hunger for learning
And an individual
      needs no guns
His faith in the Lord
      is always burning

Life takes us down
      some hard roads
But if we keep
      hope and believing
Someday Love
      will take hold
Trust the good in your heart
      and freedom you will be seeing.

POCKET IN THE WIND

The Wind always carries
    a song
Though it is not the same
    in each stay
Today I hear here voice
    so strong
Singing of the light
    of day

This peaceful harmony
    she holds
And the story that
    is told
With gray skies
    and warm rain
I listen to her
    strong refrain

How did she learn
    so many melodies
I guess her years
    they did teach
But today she sings
    of good to come
It's riding on her wings
    as she runs

So many changes
       she does tell
As water on the creek
       does swell
The frog's voices carry
       far and strong
As their chorus
       rides on

The Wind
       as she holds the birds in flight
They look as if they're
       out for a ride
Cause if you can find
       a pocket of hers to ride
Strength it will stand firmly
       at your side

As you sail on her
       mission unknown
Never doubting the
       stories she's told
You'll find the comfort
       of her embrace
Her warmth with you
       it stays

Cause the Wind
   she's been here before
And she knows what
   may be in store
Years immeasurable she's
   journeyed this Earth
Knows her from the
   day of birth

So listen to the Wind
   in your stay
She will always
   guide you on your way.

A TREE'S ESSENCE

I watch the Wind
      rustling the leaves
With their youth
      she does tease
So much they have seen
      in their short stay
More to come
      many adventures before them lay

They will grow and change
      and give necessities to life
To their brothers
      on their essence they rely
But carelessly
      man drops trees to the ground
In clear cut regions
      not a trace to be found

But how will we breathe
      when they are gone
Don't they see
      their mission is wrong
No
      money means more to many
They believe of trees
      there are plenty

Cause some they see
        only with eyes
As this sad Earth
        she cries
And those who see
        with their hearts
A mission they pursue
        a grassroots spark

To save the trees
        for they are life
Their execution
        is not right
I only hope this
        plea is heard
Cause they're the one
        who'll save this world.

PERSPECTIVE

Sometimes you are standing
        in just the right place
And the morning light
        is shining at a perfect angle
Of doubt and misunderstandings
        it will erase
Life's journey will not look
        as if in a tangle

A few days of change
        and indecision
Will shade the scenery
        the colors run
But life sets you
        in this perfect setting
So once again your
        vision will be getting

Perspective
        of everything in your life
It all stands clearly
        in front of your eyes
The past and present
        at you are staring
And this road you've chosen
        the life you're bearing

All come together
        in one moment
As if a storyteller
        had told it
An outside look at
        who you are
The road you've traveled
        come so far

And a new journey
        no longer causes doubt
You've seen your life
        has somehow worked out
So you travel on with
        strong faith
That this life you hold
        it is your fate

And missions you will
        have to live
Will only add to this
        picture life gives
Travel fearlessly
        heaven's on your side
Enjoy this life
        with the Wind you ride.

THE RAIN

The rain
      it inspires with its nourishment
The rain
      gets your feet a little wet
And I can't imagine life
      without rain
It just wouldn't
      be the same

Blue skies every day
No clouds to come your way
To shelter you from the sky
Sometimes we need the time to stay inside

And listen to the rain as she sings
All the songs of life she brings
Sometimes seems unending in her plight
But from her journey she shows a light

And those storms that pass with forceful speed
The Earth must have a need
To release its energy in rain
Thunder lightning and hurricanes

Or she couldn't survive
Sometimes tears she must cry
To clear fears away
Seems sometimes they come her way

Yes the rain
     she so inspires
And of her
     I pray I never tire
Cause the Earth needs
     her time to heal
As do her children here
     whose thirst is real.

SUN'S JOURNEY

You come creeping up
    in the morning
Bright colors
    giving warning
Proclaiming the
    break of day
Never knowing
    ahead what lay

Then as your
    brilliant appearance
Shows its beauty
    so fearless
You make your way
    through the sky
Colors vanish
    before our eyes

And spend your days
    in variation
Then for evening
    make preparation
And as you drop to
    put on another show
Sinking on the horizon
    so low
Finally fading as
    the sky grows dark
Another journey
    to embark.

MOVING WITH THE RIVER

We begin
        as an idea
And where we go
        from there is fate
Then in the end
        we will see a
Reflection
        of that initial gate

The circle
        we come and go
In between
        our seeds we sow
And where we came from
        we don't know
But in the end
        the River flows

The River of life
        keeps on moving
Changing course
        a mission pursuing
Rolling swiftly
        on its way
Sometimes slowing down
        to play

And I look at
          all the changes
We go through
          so much rearranging
A simple turn
          up ahead
Can't see beyond
          the bend

But it's always
          thought provoking
Looking ahead
          a fire stoking
Anticipation of what
          we can't see
This winding River
          so carefree

And I wonder why
          we worry
So many folks
          in a hurry
Cause life begins
          flows and ends
Adventures it always
          sends

The River
        I will follow her course
Without feeling
        remorse
Cause she knows
        she moves along
And never feels
        it is wrong

I'll accompany her
        where she goes
With the River
        I'll flow
Find life's journey
        so soothing
As long as I keep with
        the River moving.

EACH MOMENT

Time, you move on your way
Seems it's always the break of day
Moments, we miss so much time
Of beauty when we rush our lives

Last, we never know when it will come
That moment when our life is done
Lord, help me take each moment in sight
And live the most that I might
Because we don't know when that time comes
When we no longer see the morning sun

So if I seem a bit in a hurry
And sometimes my mind it worries
Send me a sign of peace in the air
So I will stop to listen and care

To the life that is around me
And the beauty it sends me
Breathing each second
Not taking for granted

The life it was given
Enjoying this moment from heaven
Let me feel that song
So I will not wrong
This life you gave me
Open my eyes to its beauty.

SEEDS PLANTED FROM THE HEART

A Tree stands strong
        waving its life in the winds
Last of a dying breed
        what will we do when it ends
Its life gives so much
        to the Earth
No price can be placed
        on its worth

And a Human passes
        through my life
With the same character
        as the tree before my eyes
Touching many, giving life
        and love to those he sees
Makes life in his world a
        place with more harmony

But the pain and burden
        he must bear
Standing alone, will someone
        feel and care

For the work he's strived
    so hard to maintain
He now wants to leave
    but will it remain
The same strong bond
    rooted like a tree
Once he's gone a piece missing
    from a family

The tree gives oxygen
    fertilizer and more life
We take it for granted
    always in our sight
If it left could we
    fill the gap
What the tree has given
    will show more when it's passed

Sometimes the seeds we've planted
    are hard to see
Not until we've stepped away
    and let them be
The strength it's given
    is not always clearly seen
Until we let the young
    carry on and live free

This Human has touched
      so many lives
His disappearance from them
      like cataracts to their eyes
But the picture of him
      they wear in their hearts
Will always remain, the seeds he's planted
      will never part.

LAST ADVENTURE

You've gotten yourself
        into situations before
But always found
        a way to escape
This time
        they're breathing down your door
There's no way out
        this may be your fate

You planned
        your strategies so well
Always found
        a way to get out
But right now
        you feel the fire of hell
In your mind
        you must feel some doubt

Looking from way up high
        you must have felt free
But then you found
        yourself trapped
And there was no way
        to flee
In your haste
        this mission was not mapped

But there's always a chance
        for survival
Though at this moment
        things look bleak
Maybe you're praying
        for its arrival
Your heart out loud
        it must now speak

And how does it feel
        to have reached this point
You've always been
        a free Spirit
Does your body freeze
        at each joint
Or do you still feel
        no fear in it

No I can't watch
        this episode
Cause it may
        be your last
The suspense is about
        to explode
Your life could be
        history past

If there was
>a way I could help

You know I'd be
>at your side

But your situation
>all outs it's stealth

This may be the last
>of your ride

So I'll step away
>and remember your charm

You had a way
>with all you touched

You'd never cause
>anyone harm

Though sometimes your presence
>could cause a hush

As the night falls
>I may hear the sound

Of your parting
>in the distance

But your memory
>will always be found

Safe in my heart
>in an instant.

REAL ESTATE FOR SALE

We found ice on the moon
And hope to settle there soon
Cause the damage we've done here
Has left folks with the fear

That the Earth can no longer sustain
Life if humans remain
On this course of destruction
The Earth in seduction

So off they'll fly
Those with money to buy
A ticket to the moon
And real estate too
They'll divide the land
Melt the ice so they can
Have water for drink
That ice they will shrink

And hope there's enough
'Til to another planet they can thrust
Their spaceships so they can survive
Humans have brains that can devise
Ways of changing life to their needs
To fill their hunger on it they'll feed

So though some may fear
That human life's end is near
No need to worry
Those pocket books will surely
Buy life on another planet
Maybe a home on Saturn
Perhaps then the meek will inherit the Earth
And respect it for its worth
Though years may go by 'til it heals
Again its beauty and love warm hearts will feel.

FULL MOON

The Moon's coming up
     over the Lake
Of its presence
     you make no mistake
Staring boldly
     into the night
Effortlessly climbing
     in its flight

Makes me wonder
     how the world feels tonight
Something in the air
     is not quite right
But I'll let it pass
     this moment of doubt
Send the feeling
     sailing out

Cause when the Moon
     shows her face
There's a feeling
     you can't erase
She stirs you
     from inside
Takes your senses
     for a ride

And if you go along
       with her whim
Enjoy her stay
       and let her in
She'll bring you places
       not usually seen
Guide you with
       her fearless beams

And at the
       break of dawn
You feel her presence
       is gone
But the picture she laid
       before your eyes
Of which she made
       no disguise

Is a vision
       you'll always keep
Leaves a message
       so deep.

RAINBOW IN THE STORM

Sometimes when
      your life is in disarray
And your dreams
      have gone away
Your world
      seems to shatter
As each day
      you try to gather
Pieces of order
      back together
And find
      even stormier weather

The days soon
      turn to night
Sometimes looking
      for something right
But in this dismay
      you'll find light
In the strangest places
      stands hope in your sight
And it'll touch your soul
      deep inside
Bring you back
      to friendly tides
To make your world of despair
      seem to end
A beautiful rainbow
      it will send

And though its stay
        may be brief
Will bring you back
        a belief
That good
        will come your way
Will open its door
        to you someday

And the dark
        will disappear
In the distance
        you will hear
Its message
        to love your life
Every passage
        must feel some strife
It builds strength
        in our souls
Though in its time
        takes its toll

But the beauty
        of our being
Would somehow
        be hard to see
If all of life
        were sunny days
And storms
        never came our way.

YELLOW DAISIES

The field so bright
      serenity it does release
Any tension you feel
      it will cease
A calm
      as a Southwest Wind blows
This early September day
      it knows

How to lullaby
      a crying child
Put their head
      to rest for a while
She has that way
      about her knowing
The easiness in the air
      she's sowing

And butterflies
      they float with ease
On this cool
      Southwest breeze
Touching each flower
      without a sound
On every pedal
      can be found

Brilliance
      as the sun shines bright
This picture
      a dazzling yellow sight
Causing eyes
      to rest easy
With their beauty
      they are teasing

Cause they must know
      of their charm
A look will tell you
      they will not harm
As they circle
      a purple field
Young Poplars
      from their center yield

And dance
      in their warm surroundings
So much life
      is abounding
Where months ago
      a frog's serenade
And young ducklings
      did parade

Life
      in the dawning of a creek
Year round
      its journey does speak.

IF A SEED REMAINS

Will you remember me
        when I'm gone
When humans have done
        the Earth too much wrong
And the air
        it will not sustain
Our lungs
        and tainted water's all that remains

Will you someday
        send up a seed
And maybe in your thoughts
        you'll see
Me sitting at this
        chair by dawn
And writing verse
        perhaps a song

Will you wish the humans
        would have stayed
Maybe a few of us
        could have found a way
To make the Earth
        a peaceful place
And found ourselves
        an untouched space

Oh I hope there is
    a spot around
Where Life and Love
    will abound
And perhaps the children
    God has chosen
In their hearts
    will not be woven

That string that gives
    us greed and hate
That thread will have
    met its fate
And died with all
    the wrong and evil
Never again
    this Earth to fill

Possessions that will
    make us destroy
Our own habitat
    to bring materialistic joy
Yes the Earth will fill
    with Love
Things God sent us
    from above

And the Tree will stand
        tall and proud
No chain saw to drop them
        to the ground
Peace will hold
        the Earth together
Without fear
        or warring weather

Hope
        is there still a trace
Oh wise seed
        do you see this place
Or do you shutter
        with a fear
We will repeat
        our mistakes here

Give us a chance
        let us make
A peaceful world
        just one place it would take

On that wonderful
        sunny morning
When your seed has sprouted
        to a seedling
Take a look around
        and tell me
How the Earth feels
        with no greed.

CLONED TO THE BONE

I'll take
      two copies
One for my girlfriend
      and one for my wife
And please
      don't get sloppy
I want those clones
      to have my eyes

How could this world get along
      without me
I've wondered how
      it would be
But they've found a way
      to make a copy
So today I'll go
      clone shopping

Be careful
      with that cell
And remember it must *almost* die
      but don't send it to hell
Be careful where
      you incubate
A Mother no longer
      is just fate

Find me one
        who's understanding
Loves me unconditionally
        with perfect handling
No need to keep those photos
        from when I'm a baby
They'll send me back around
        just by paying

Oh Cloning
        at last I've found
A way to keep
        this old body around
And I can be in more than
        one place at a time
I may commit
        the perfect crime

Human discoveries
        they persist in finding
Ways to keep
        this old Earth crying.

LOOKING AT LIFE FROM A LILY PAD

If Frogs
    could fly
I'd look
    from up high
And watch
    as the miles went by

But Frogs
    they hop
Gravity
    does stop
Us from viewing
    life on top

Though we enjoy
    our limbs
They move us
    with vim
Across the water
    we can skim

We make the most
    of our gifts
With long tongues
    we can lift
A fly from the air
    with the tip

And supper
        is not far away
On a humid
        Summer day
So many bugs
        they pass our way

But skill
        it takes
For a Frog
        to make
A meal of a bug
        on the lake

But Lily Pads
        disguise
So we can
        hide
And sometimes they
        land at our side

Though the thought
        of flying is appealing
So much of the
        Earth revealing
But life from the ground
        can give feeling

With close encounters
       to many things
Crickets chirping
       and birds that sing
Together
       their voices ring

In unison
And we join in
Serenading on a whim

Yes looking at life
       from a lily pad
So much perception
       to be had
Colors around camouflage
       as in Earthly colors we're clad

And though up in the air
       looks tempting
This amphibian life
       will keep me inventing
Verse from the Earth
       with the inspiration it's sending.

100% LIFE RECYCLED INTO VERSE
ON 100% RECYCLED PAPER